Here Comes Tricky Rabbit!

Other Books by Gretchen Will Mayo

*Star Tales: North American Indian Stories
About the Stars*

*Earthmaker's Tales: North American Indian
Stories About Earth Happenings*

Meet Tricky Coyote!

That Tricky Coyote!

Big Trouble for Tricky Rabbit!

Illustrated by Gretchen Will Mayo

Whale Brother

Native American Trickster Tales

Here Comes Tricky Rabbit!

Retold and Illustrated by
Gretchen Will Mayo

Walker and Company New York

This book is dedicated to Sharron St. John, in celebration of her gift for untangling life stories.

First published in the United States of America in 1994
by Walker Publishing Company, Inc.

Published simultaneously in Canada by Thomas Allen and Sons Canada, Limited, Markham, Ontario

Library of Congress Cataloging-in-Publication Data
Mayo, Gretchen.
Here comes tricky rabbit! / retold and illustrated by Gretchen Will Mayo.
p.   cm.
Includes bibliographical references.
ISBN 0-8027-8273-6. —ISBN 0-8027-8274-4 (lib. bdg.)
1. Indians of North America—Legends.   2. Rabbits—Folklore.
3. Trickster—Juvenile literature.   I. Title.
E98.F6M342 1994
398.2'08997—dc20   93-29763
CIP
AC

The art for *Here Comes Tricky Rabbit!* was painted with opaque acrylics on watercolor board.

Book design by Brandon Kruse

Printed in Hong Kong

2 4 6 8 10 9 7 5 3 1

Contents

v

Acknowledgments

Many people and institutions helped me generously when I researched the Rabbit stories and pictures. I send thanks and admiration to Dr. Jay Miller, D'Arcy McNickle Center for the History of the American Indian, the Newberry Library, Chicago; the Milwaukee Public Museum and its library staff (especially Judy Turner); the Kansas City Public Library; the University of Wisconsin system for use of its libraries; Joseph Bruchac, Abenaki storyteller and author; Amelia Cornelius, Oneida storyteller and author.

I am especially grateful to Margaret Jensen, whose understanding of young children and whose expertise in the early reader's process has contributed greatly to the crafting of this book.

Here Comes Tricky Rabbit!

Clear the way!
Here comes Tricky Rabbit.
Yes, he's small,
but don't be fooled.
Some say he killed a hungry giant
bigger than a mountain.
Some say he once trapped the sun.
That was back when Earth was young.
Now who will Rabbit trick today?

Fancy Dancing

Oh, no! Rabbit was in a terrible fix! Wolf and his friends had him trapped. They looked at Rabbit and licked their lips.

Rabbit looked back. He tapped his foot on the ground while he thought. Tap, tap-tap, tap! Then Rabbit smiled and said, "You have come at the right time, my friends. I was just going to try my new dance."

"Who cares!" Wolf growled. "I'm hungry."

"Suit yourself," said Rabbit, but he tap-tap-tapped his other foot.

"Hold on!" cried one of the wolves. "I hear Rabbit is a great dancer. I want to see what he can do."

"Grrrrrr!" said Wolf, but all his friends made a circle around Rabbit.

Rabbit tap-tap-tapped some more and gave a sly smile. "If you watch me, I will teach you the dance. It is a dance you will never forget." Rabbit smiled. "But you must help me."

"Get on with it," grumbled Wolf. "What do we have to do?"

Rabbit said, "The dancing song goes like this: Ha' nia lil, lil! Ha' nia lil, lil! Whenever I sing 'lil, lil!' you must stomp your feet." Rabbit stomped his feet hard. Stomp, stomp. "Now you try it," said Rabbit.

"That's simple!" cried Wolf. He stomped his feet. Stomp, stomp. His friends stomped their feet too. "What is the rest of the dance?" called Wolf.

"Watch me," said Rabbit. "Ha' nia lil, lil!" sang Rabbit as he danced. The wolves

stomped their feet at just the right time.

"Good work!" called Rabbit. "This time I will add more words. You will have to stomp more times. Listen carefully!"

All the wolves listened.

"Ha' nia lil, lil, lil, lil!" Rabbit sang. He danced away from the middle. The wolves stomp-stomp-stomp-stomped.

"What great dancers you are!" shouted Rabbit. "You are ready for harder steps."

"Hey! This is fun!" cried the wolves. "Show us more, Rabbit!"

"Okay! This time turn around when you

stomp your feet," said Rabbit.

"Ha' nia lil, lil, lil, lil, lil, lil." Each time Rabbit sang "lil," he danced a little farther away. The wolves stomped their feet a little harder. "Lil, lil, lil." Stomp and turn, stomp and turn, stomp and turn.

"Make room for Rabbit!" cried Wolf as he stomped and turned.

The wolves opened the circle to make room for Rabbit.

"Ha' nia lil, lil, lil, lil." Rabbit twirled out of the circle.

"Lil, lil, lil, lil." The wolves stomped and turned.

"Lil, lil, lil, lil." Rabbit danced and twirled around the dancing wolves.

"Lil, lil, lil." Stomp, stomp, stomp. Then Rabbit made a big jump and disappeared into the tall grass.

"Where is Rabbit?" cried Wolf. "Where is our dancing teacher?"

"Ha' nia lil, lil, lil!" yelled Rabbit from the tall grass. "Don't stop. Keep dancing!"

"Right on!" shouted Wolf. Wolf and his friends stomped and turned. They twirled and swirled while Rabbit sang.

But then Rabbit's singing stopped.

"Don't stop. Keep singing!" Wolf called to

Rabbit.

But Rabbit didn't sing.

"Rabbit, where are you?" hollered Wolf. Everyone listened. They heard only the wind blowing through the tall grass.

"Oh, no!" yelled Wolf. "Rabbit is gone."

All the wolves dashed into the tall grass. They looked and looked for Rabbit. They found only his footprints running through the tall grass.

Wolf stamped his foot. "We let Rabbit twirl right out of our trap," he grumbled.

James Wafford heard the Cherokee story about Rabbit fooling the wolves while working in Indian territory. In the late 1890s Wafford reported the story to James Mooney, who recorded it for the U.S. Bureau of Ethnology.

Me Too!

Rabbit watched Otter in the pond. What a swimmer! Otter could dive without a splash. Without a ripple Otter reached up and caught a duck for dinner.

"I can do that!" thought Rabbit. "I can catch a duck for dinner too." First Rabbit

made a rope for himself. Then he called to Otter, "Watch me!" and Rabbit jumped into the water with his rope.

Rabbit kicked. He splashed. He made a lot of noise in the water. Some of the ducks flew away. Rabbit heard Otter laughing on the shore.

"Who cares," said Rabbit. "I will dive under just like Otter. Then the ducks won't see me. I will tie my rope to a duck's foot. I can catch a duck for dinner too, just like Otter."

Rabbit took a deep breath. He dove down, down. He paddled over to the ducks. No one knew he was there. "See! Just like Otter," thought Rabbit.

Rabbit swam under the ducks. He looked up at the duck's feet in the water. "So many ducks!" thought Rabbit. "Which one will I choose?" Rabbit thought again. "Otter has only one duck for dinner. I could have lots of ducks. Then everyone will say, 'Rabbit is the best duck hunter of all!'"

Quickly Rabbit wrapped his rope around one duck's foot. Then another. Then another. Rabbit jerked the rope tight.

Quack! Quack! Quack! Quack!

Rabbit had so many ducks on his rope. What a feast he would have.

But the ducks did not want to be a feast.

Together they flap-flapped their wings. Together they rose from the water. Together they pulled Rabbit right along with them into the sky.

"Stop!" yelled Rabbit. "I am not a bird, I am a rabbit! Let me down!"

On the pond Otter laughed and laughed. "Bye-bye!" he called.

The ducks did not stop. They flew over the bushes. They flew over the hill. They flew far away from the pond.

Rabbit was tired. He could not hold on to the rope any longer. He fell down, down, out of the sky. He landed in the hollow trunk of a tree.

Now Rabbit was trapped. He could not jump high enough. He could not get out of the hollow tree trunk.

"Help!" shouted Rabbit. "Help, help!"

Lucky for Rabbit, someone came along. It was Woodpecker. Peck-peck-peck. Woodpecker pecked at the hollow tree. Woodpecker was looking for bugs to eat. Peck-peck-peck.

"Hey! I am not a bug!" called Rabbit. "Stop making all that noise."

Woodpecker stopped. "Who is in there?" she called.

"Someone beautiful," said Rabbit.

"I can hear you, but I cannot see you," said Woodpecker. "I would like to see you."

"Make a hole. Then you can see," said Rabbit.

Peck-peck-peck. Woodpecker made a hole. "I see your eye. I cannot see more," said Woodpecker.

"Make the hole bigger," called Rabbit. "Then I will show you how beautiful I am."

Woodpecker pecked and pecked.

Ho-hum. Rabbit was tired of waiting.

Finally he called, "Get out of the way. I am coming out. It's time to show you how beautiful I am."

Woodpecker said, "The hole isn't very big."

"Who cares?!" said Rabbit. He squeezed into the hole. He squashed through. He left behind a lot of rabbit hair.

"Thanks!" said Rabbit, and then he ran away.

"You don't look very beautiful to me!" called Woodpecker.

Stories about Rabbit's duck hunting troubles are popular among the people of the Cherokee, Creek, Koasati, and Alabama nations. John Ax, Suyeta, James Wafford, and the famous Cherokee storyteller Swimmer were among those whose Rabbit stories were recorded around 1900.

Bobcat

Hoppity-hoppity-hoppity-hoppity. Rabbit raced across the field.

Pa-dum, pa-dum, pa-dum, pa-dum. Bobcat raced after Rabbit.

Bobcat was hungry.

Rabbit was scared. But Rabbit was smart. He dashed to a hollow tree. He squeezed

into a little hole. "Ha ha!" Rabbit laughed. "Now you can't get me. The hole is too small for you, Bobcat."

"Ha ha!" Bobcat laughed. "You thought you were smart, Rabbit. But now you are trapped.

You will get hungry. You will come out to eat. I will be here."

Bobcat waited outside.

Rabbit waited inside. But Rabbit was busy. He found two acorns Squirrel had left behind. Then he called to Bobcat, "Okay. You win. I am coming out."

"It's about time," said Bobcat.

"Hold on. I have one last wish before you eat me," said Rabbit. "Even Rabbits should have one last wish."

"Let's hear your wish," said Bobcat. His stomach growled.

Rabbit called, "I want to be a dinner you will never forget. You must build a fire. You must roast me until I am tender. Then you will say, 'That Rabbit, I will never forget him!'"

"Wow," said Bobcat. "You have a big heart, Rabbit! You deserve to have your wish." So Bobcat gathered lots of dry grass and twigs. He piled them right in front of Rabbit's hole. Then he started the fire.

"It's getting hot in here," said Rabbit in a loud voice.

Bobcat blew on the fire to make it bigger.

"Hot, hot, hot!" called Rabbit in his loudest voice.

Bobcat thought about his dinner. He blew on the fire some more.

Rabbit yelled, "I'm so hot that my eyes are popping out."

Then Rabbit threw one of the acorns out of the hole. "There goes one eye," he called.

Pop! The acorn landed in the fire and burst into flame.

"Oh no! There goes my other eye," Rabbit yelled.

Pop! The second acorn landed in the fire and burst into flame.

"Rabbit, what is going on?" called Bobcat.

"My eyes popped out. I can't see." Rabbit lied. "You will have to come close, Bobcat. You will have to help me come out."

Bobcat came close. "Come on out, Rabbit. I will help you. I am ready for a dinner I will

never forget," called Bobcat.

Rabbit jumped out of the hole. But he did not let Bobcat help. Swish! Rabbit kicked the fire with his big back feet. Sparks flew. Hot coals flew. They landed all over Bobcat.

"Ouch!" yelled Bobcat. He beat the sparks on his coat. He jumped. He rolled in the dust.

Rabbit ran away.

Bobcat brushed away the dust and looked at his coat. It was covered with spots.

Rabbit was right. Bobcat will never forget him. Now, because of tricky Rabbit, Bobcat and all his grandchildren wear spotted coats.

Both the Kickapoo and the Shawnee tell stories explaining how Bobcat, also known as Wildcat, got his spots. A version told by Charles Bluejacket was recorded around 1859 when he was a leader of the Shawnee nation. Charles Bluejacket was born in 1816 along the Huron River in Michigan. For many years when he was young, Charles worked as an interpreter. His last name, Bluejacket, came from his grandfather, who was a famous warrior chief.

Rabbit's Toothache

Rabbit did not know Coyote was near.

He did not see Coyote tiptoe, tiptoe up behind him. But just when Coyote was ready to jump, Rabbit turned around.

Coyote! There he was with his big, hungry mouth!

Rabbit wanted to run, but he did not. Coyote might catch him. So instead, clever Rabbit put his head between his paws.

"Ow! Ow! Owwwwwwwww!" he cried.

Coyote stopped to listen. "Rabbit, why are you singing?" asked Coyote.

"Owwwwwwww. I'm not singing," answered Rabbit. "My tooth hurts. Owwwwwwww!"

"Too bad," said Coyote. "Maybe I can help you. Maybe I can bring something to make your tooth feel better." Coyote's words sounded sweet, but Coyote wasn't sweet. He was making plans to trick Rabbit.

"Rabbit looks mighty tasty," thought

Coyote. "I will promise to bring Rabbit something to make his tooth feel better. Then he won't run away. He will be an easy catch for my lunch." Coyote's smile grew bigger.

Rabbit gave Coyote a sad look and said, "Thank you for your offer, Coyote. You are a true friend."

Coyote thought, "Hee, hee, hee! What a dummy! Rabbits are my favorite lunch."

Rabbit thought, "Hee, hee, hee! I'm no dummy! If I wait here for Coyote, he will turn me into rabbit stew."

As soon as Coyote turned away, Rabbit

24

jumped into a hole in the ground. It was very dark in there. It was not very quiet.

A voice inside was shouting at Rabbit. "This is *not* a rabbit hole. This is a *skunk* hole. What are you doing in my house?"

"Oops! Sorry, Skunk," said Rabbit. "Coyote thinks he can trick me. He thinks I will make a tasty lunch. I jumped in here to hide."

"Smart kid!" said Skunk. Then she looked out the hole and said, "Here comes that tricky Coyote now."

Coyote ran with his nose to the ground. Sniff! Sniff! Sniff! He followed Rabbit's footprints right up to Skunk's hole. Sniff! Sniff! Sniff! "Hey, down there!" called Coyote. "Anybody home?"

"Just me," answered Skunk.

"Anybody else?" asked Coyote.

"Nobody else." Skunk lied.

Coyote ran around sniff-sniffing some more. He looked at Rabbit's tracks. He saw where they went. Then he dashed back to

Skunk's hole. "I don't believe you, Skunk!"
Coyote shouted. "I'll bet Rabbit is with you."

"If you don't believe me, look for yourself,"
said Skunk.

"I'll do that!" said Coyote. He leaned
down, down, into Skunk's hole.

Then Skunk turned around. She lifted her

long, bushy tail and . . . Pssssssst! Pssssssst!
P.U.!

"Gotcha!" yelled Skunk.

"Yuck!" yelled Coyote.

What a stink!

Now Coyote smells worse than rotten meat.

Now even the flies won't sit on Coyote.

Now Rabbit always knows when Coyote is near.

P.U.!

Both the Apache, who call themselves the Dineh (meaning "The People"), and the Tiwa of Taos pueblo in New Mexico tell stories of Rabbit's toothache. Apache bow hunters once ranged across New Mexico and Arizona, but many were forced into reservations in New Mexico during the late 1800s. Today Apaches run successful businesses while carrying on traditional values and ceremonies.

No! No! Not That!

The creeks were dry. The river was dry.
Everyone was thirsty. "We need a well," said
Fox. So everyone worked together to dig a
well. It was hard work.

Lazy Rabbit did not help.

Fox said, "If you don't help, you can't
share."

"Who cares! I don't need a well," said
Rabbit. "I can lick the dew from the grass
instead."

"What a dreamer," said Fox.

No one believed Rabbit.

After the well was finished, someone said, "I saw Rabbit with a pot full of water. Where did he find so much dew?"

"I think Rabbit is a thief," said Fox. "I think he takes water from our well when we are sleeping."

So Fox made a guard for their well. He made the guard of twigs and clay. He covered it with sticky tar. When he was finished the guard looked just like a wolf. Fox leaned the tar wolf on the well.

When everyone was asleep, Rabbit ran to the well. He carried a big pot. But Tar Wolf was in his way.

"Who are you?" asked Rabbit.

The tar wolf did not speak.

"Why don't you say something?" asked Rabbit.

The tar wolf said nothing.

"Don't be stubborn!" said Rabbit.

Tar Wolf stayed silent as a stone.

"Well, get out of my way, whoever you are," snapped Rabbit. He reached out to shove the tar wolf away. Rabbit's fist stuck tight.

"Give me back my hand!" said Rabbit. He hit Tar Wolf with his other hand. Now both of Rabbit's hands were stuck.

"Let me go!" called Rabbit. He kicked Tar

Wolf with one back foot and then the other. Poor Rabbit! He was stuck to the tar wolf like a feather sticks to glue.

Morning came. Everyone woke up. A surprise was waiting at the well. There was Rabbit, still stuck to the tar wolf.

"What should we do with this thief?" asked Fox. "We must teach him a lesson."

Rabbit thought, "I don't like the sound of this."

Everyone shouted, "Throw him into the fire!"

Rabbit thought, "I don't like the sound of this one bit!" He was scared. But Rabbit didn't cry. Rabbit put on a big smile instead. Then he laughed. "Yes! Yes! Yes! Please! Throw me into the fire! I'm so happy when I'm hot!" Rabbit lied.

"No way! We'll throw you into the well instead," someone called.

"Yes! Yes! Yes! Throw me into the well. I love to swim!" Rabbit lied.

Fox growled. "We don't want to make you

happy, Rabbit. We want to teach you a lesson."

Then Rabbit's smile turned into a frown. He began to cry.

"What's wrong?" asked Fox.

"I'm afraid." Rabbit sobbed. "I'm afraid you will throw me into the thorny thicket."

"What a great idea," said Fox. "We will throw you into the thicket. That will teach you a lesson you will not forget."

"No, no! Not that!" cried Rabbit. "Not the thicket. Throw me anywhere but the thicket!"

"Too bad, Rabbit," said Fox. "You brought this trouble on yourself."

So they carried Rabbit off.

"No, no! Not there!" yelled Rabbit.

They threw Rabbit right into the middle of the thicket.

Rabbit jumped up right where he landed. Then he laughed and laughed.

"Thank you, thank you, thank you, friends," called Rabbit. "This is the nicest lesson I've ever had. The thicket is my home, you know." Clever Rabbit ran away.

The rivalry between Rabbit and Fox has long been celebrated by storytellers from this land and others. Some say the Tar Baby stories were brought to the North American continent by African slaves. Others say the American Indians told these stories even before Europeans invaded Indian lands. Perhaps over time stories from both cultures were blended. Between 1879 and 1913 stories about Rabbit and a tar figure were recorded from the Dineh, Biloxi, Alabama, Creek, Yuchi, and Natchez nations, among others.

Who Is Rabbit?

Rabbits are found throughout North America, from the cold arctic regions to the deserts. While their appearances vary as greatly as their environments, many characteristics are common to all. They are cute, with round eyes and soft fur, and they appear to be the most gentle, harmless of creatures. Given these features it is hard to believe that the trickster Rabbit created by American Indian storytellers could be so enduringly popular, until we remember that in life, as in the trickster tales, small and harmless does not mean incapable.

During the time of the trickster stories, every animal looked liked a human being, with head, hands, and legs. They were also subject to the same thoughts and emotions as human beings. It was only when they went outside that they put on the appearance of their species. As a character, Rabbit provided for an extended treatment of the innocuous. Through craft and trickery, he often got his way, as these stories attest. While others might misjudge him, he had the skill and confidence to best the big and humble the mighty.

Among tribes of the Great Lakes, as Manibozo or the Great Hare, Rabbit had aspects of divinity that enabled him to establish rules and traditions that people still observe. Most of the tales about Rabbit, though, focus on how he and other animals attained their looks and characteristics, and on the developing order of the world. As the stories unfolded and new stories were told, Rabbit split his lip, shortened his arms, and bent his legs. Many kinds of rabbits resulted. Most of the stories are about cottontails, but jackrabbits and arctic hares also came into their own by the time the world was finished.

The split lip so distinctive of rabbits received considerable attention in tales and everyday life. Parents were urged by their elders not to think about or look at rabbits so their baby would not be born with a harelip. Of course, some babies were born with this affliction and their parents were blamed for not paying attention to the needs of the unborn. As a result, the child got even more attention. Everything had its compensation, even disfigurement. Since American Indians lived in a world that was thoroughly interconnected, the actions of parents and of rabbits reflected on each other, but there were ways of dealing with the consequences.

The tribes of the East gave Rabbit much attention. While his flesh often appeared as dinner, his need to live was respected. People believed that rabbits would offer themselves willingly to be killed if prayers were made to explain that humans needed them for survival.

Western tribes treasured their rabbit-fur blankets during the cold winter months. Often, in Nevada and Utah, a blanket woven of strips of rabbit fur was the most valuable and useful thing a person owned. Children knew that they were adults when they were given fur blankets of their own.

In the cold North, Rabbit changed his coat with the seasons, turning white in winter. People were pleased that he was so helpful, giving them brown and white fur to decorate their clothing.

But rabbits had more to offer than themselves as food or their fur for warmth. Rabbits showed how to move through a tangle, living as they did in warrens, brambles, and undergrowth. They also lived in groups, which is how people should live. They got along with each other and raised large, happy families. They were gentle and herbivorous. Perhaps most important, their big ears show that they are careful listeners, and that may be the best lesson of all.

Jay Miller, Ph.D.,
D'Arcy McNickle Center for the History of the American Indian,
the Newberry Library, Chicago

Sources

The first people of the North American continent have a long tradition of storytelling. Often, however, their stories were recorded for the first time by non-Indians, usually scholars in the fields of anthropology and ethnology. We should always remember that these stories belong to the First People. We thank and honor those Native American Indians who shared their stories for the following reporters and publications:

Jones, William, and Michelson, Truman. "Kickapoo Tales." *9th Publication of the American Ethnological Society.* Leyden, Holland: E. J. Brill, Ltd., 1915.

Kilpatrick, Jack F., and Kilpatrick, Anna Gritts. "Cherokee Folktales: Reconstructed from the Field Notes of Franz M. Olbrechts." *196th Bulletin of the U.S. Bureau of American Ethnology.* Washington, D.C.: 1966.

Mooney, James. "Myths of the Cherokee." *19th Annual Report to the Bureau of American Ethnology.* Washington, D.C.: 1897-98.

Parsons, Elsie Clews. "Taos Tales." *Memoirs of the American Folklore Society*, vol. 34. New York: J. J. Augustin Co., 1940.

Spencer, J. "Shawnee Folk-Lore." *Journal of American Folklore* 22:323.

Swanton, John R. "Myths and Tales of the Southeastern Indians." *88th Bulletin of the Bureau of American Ethnology.* Washington, D.C.: 1929.

The following resources were consulted for background:

Current-Garcia, Eugene, ed. *Shem, Ham and Japeth: The Papers of W. O. Tuggle.* Athens: University of Georgia Press, 1973.

Dorsey, J. Owen. "Nanebozhu in Siouan Mythology." *Journal of American Folklore* 5:293-97.

Kilpatrick, Jack Frederick, and Kilpatrick, Anna Gritts. *Friends of Thunder: Folktales of the Oklahoma Cherokees.* Dallas: Southern Methodist University Press, 1964.

Lankford, George E., ed. *Native American Legends. Southeastern Legends: Tales from the Natchez, Caddo, Biloxi, Chickasaw, and Other Nations.* Little Rock: August House, 1987.